WINGED INSECTS

WINGED INSECTS

POEMS BY
JOEL LONG

WHITE PINE PRESS · BUFFALO, NEW YORK

WHITE PINE PRESS
P.O. Box 236, Buffalo, New York 14201

Acknowledgements; The following poems appeared in these magazines:
"Common Evenings," *Prairie Schooner;* "A Thousand Hats Floating," *Wisconsin Review;* "Below the Water," *The Cape Rock;* "Bone" and "Accident," *City Art;* "Learning to Speak," *Northern Lights;* "Drinking," *Galley Sail Review;* "Flavor" and "An Angel Wakes the Sleeping Magi," *Wisconsin Review;* "Iris Cut and Buried in a Hat Box" and "Brass Buttons," *Willow Springs;* "The Sacrament of Roses in Mantanzas Creek," *The MacGuffin;* "Waking with Sarah," *Mothering.*

The poem "Infant Care" will appear in an anthology on the parent and child bond from Poet Works.

I would like to thank my teachers including Mark Strand, Larry Levis, James Doyle, and Jacqueline Osherow. Thanks to Katharine Coles for helping me with the manuscript. Special thanks to Brenda Miller and Robert Hodgson Van Wagoner for their friendship, encouragement, and literary sense.

Book design: Elaine LaMattina

Printed and bound in the United States of America

1   3   5   7   9   10   8   6   4   2

Library of Congress Cataloging-in-Publication Data
Long, Joel, 1964–
Winged insects : poems / Joel Long.
p.   cm.
"1998 White Pine Press poetry prize winner"—Cover.
ISBN 1-877727-98-9 (alk. paper)
I. Title
PS3562.0494335W56   1999
811'.54–dc21   99-19084
                           CIP

For my daughters Hannah and Sarah

CONTENTS

III: *Winged Insects*

IV: *Requiem*

I.

Common Evenings

An Angel Wakes the Sleeping Magi

*After the sculpture by Gislebertus
at the Cathedral of St. Lazare at Autun*

He wakes you from a dream where you were nestled
between two countries, the wide arc of the world
embroidered of wind and gold wrapped around you.
His hand made from light drifts down the sky
and touches the skin of your hand, and all at once
the blood inside you becomes new, learns
to tell time a different way, illuminated
like a string of paper lanterns, hanging in distance.

Whole cities are destroyed and built again.
Flies increase their buzz. Rivers go dry
and roll again. Books are unwritten and rewritten.
Cows are born and relive entire lives
inside this new and sparkling globe. They graze
in fresh pastures beneath skies, living with stars.

This sweeter flood lasts an instant inside you.
All language fills with it, this new untranslatable song
we continue to hum among the dark stones of the field.

Bone

Spine bones of a deer are runes
in line on moist dirt, pine needles, grass.
They glow like stone lamps,
having had these years to shun the practice of flesh.
A vertebra in my hand becomes a mask,
too small for my face, but anxious
to cover as it has been covered,
to take its turn at making skin a shadow,
to say wildly like an expert,
"This is how it feels in the dark."

Some camper will gather these bones,
string them on twine, and hang them
in a tree like strange tinsel.
Wind will pass over them,
and the ivory tongues will rattle
and tell the many versions at once
of what it's like to be inside.

Common Evenings

The deer crashed through your window
under the illusion of nothing
solid in the air in front of her, for fear makes us
run through everything and finally stop to tremble
among the shards of broken glass and strange furniture.

When all is normal,
the child dressing for bed, the father
reading the paper, and the mother with her hand
down the drain, feeling for spoons in the carrot peels,
something extraordinary happens.
A plane explodes.
A chicken pecks a wet hole through brown shell.
A cow in the dung lets out a scream beneath a half-moon.
The sidewalk is cold and still.
A woman with a mole on her collarbone conceives.

And that deer, sitting in your living room
with a gash under her eye, burst inside
the common evening to disturb your dinner conversation
and wind your hearts into a flutter spin.
How quickly we become smoke, trailing luxurious lines on the air,
descending with the white porcelain of the sugar bowl
into exotic spiralings of molecules.
We marvel at these moments and the objects moving through,
the doe backing into the ottoman, a kiss on the open eye.

Beating the Shark

When the shark happened into waters
too shallow,
the swimmers headed for shore, screaming his name.

They looked back to see his lethargic fin
tilting above water
like an empty bag, like slow steam.

They ventured toward him, splashing the sea side
of him. He moved closer
to shore. They moved closer to him, slapping

the water with float tubes, with the bare
flat of their hands
until the shark's belly hit sand, and he panicked,

and he rolled, flipped his tail in the air
and twisted his rough body
until it wrinkled at its crease. He fell back.

The swimmers, feeling safe, drew near enough
to touch him,
to push him, to roll him over like driftwood

with eyes, which on either side could likely see
the nothing floating in
like haze. A man with a bandanna tied around

his head came from shore with a fence post
and began beating
the head of the shark with blows that sounded

like blurred, distant hammers building the frame of a house.
Others came behind him
with sticks and beat down on the shark,

and with each blow, his eyes rotated wildly
in their orbits, and a bit
of air hissed out between those famous and white teeth.

They beat him, threw Coke bottles at him, kicked him
long after the shark
was dead. If it had been dark, the bodies

of these bathers would have lit up like neon,
like sparks from wires
with all the pleasure of each hit against the darkness,

against that fearful, sharp mouth and its gullet. It sizzled.
It burst. It was the center
of all force. Perhaps they thought this would make them

feel somehow better, that something small would lift
from them like a black
inner tongue, that when they looked up

from the misshapen body, the day around them would—
in the flat, apparent noon—
be less filled with the common threat inside them all.

The Iris Cut and Buried in a Hat Box

The iris is a floating thing there
underground. It is a star of different design,
violet music seeping outward.
An endless snake slides its cool belly
across cello strings, the bright
chord of a mouthless spirit, chanting.
Three spines of iris soft-arched and pungent.
Sweet air, private and whole
hovers like a slow swarm of light,
churning away from and about the flower,
suspending it in the dark. It is a purple weather, a wind
preserved, glowing like a woman
with the sun in her mouth or like a poison
gas alone. It is the damp skeleton of joy, thinking
it is the only thing.

From the Ebbo Gospels

Matthew dips his pen in silk and trouble,
and the words spill out like fishes
into the terrible dark, illuminated with frenzy.
The wind from his eyes sets the land in motion,
begins the strange descent of the bite-sized angel
who pours the spirits, thick as fumes,
into his ears, and Matthew begins to float.

These buildings and all are air, he thinks,
made of the mortar of where the swallows flew
and this chair, with the grace and love of things,
lifts itself toward the center of the sky.
Matthew forms his body to the shape of the word
like an electric bit of clay or a blue snake entranced,
cool beneath the invisible hands that hold it.

Skunk Poem

From what meadow will it come,
wet with underlife, smelling
of decay as though it survived
the millennium holding its breath beneath
sticks and mud? It should not be unlike
a baby skunk, fresh from the womb,
blind and unprepared for a world of any kind.
Like Lao Tzu's clay pots, they cannot hold themselves up,
and therefore, they are perfect when they collapse,
perfect when somehow in that new darkness
they find the mother skunk's teat
and begin sucking their way
into the light, which will lift them,
which will make them more
like the animal they are.

A Thousand Hats Floating

A thousand hats floated in the sea,
and the car keys dropped as expected, deep
like metallic and insane birds.
Yellow and blue schools of fish watched,
quietly amazed at all the commotion,
the waving arms, the kicking,
the water screams, and the money
floating from wallets like wet kites.

It was a day for water
to remember, all that consciousness
dissolved like boats of crystal sugar,
the sweet sea churning with thought,
churning with the last, thousand moments
of terror, each as horrifying as being
in this world can be, each intricate
and precise.

On the Eve of Your Surgery

for Jude

You know what it is to clip
the unbloomed rose
that hardens and dries
like the swallow's skull,
to pluck out the tulip
whose petals have curled over
like the lips of a girl in seizure
to expose the awful
yellow tongue and black teeth,
misarranged about it.

These flowers were meant
to dazzle, and so you arrange them
to set a galaxy in motion,
all turning on the vertical throat
of the calla lily
and a spray of angel's breath.
Here, loss is hidden
or postponed.
Flowers speed back into time
only more quickly, with greater brilliance,
the orchid like the secret organ
of an imaginary fish
glowing among the tall grass.

How to Remember Windows

for my mother

The whole scene seems suspended
in silk curtains, not silk exactly—

it scratched my skin—translucent
veil for a window, sweeping the hardwood by the bed

as I breathed. When I was four, I knew that time was an opening,
a crystal wait and foolish looking for you, at the empty

curbside beneath the tree with knobs. At the wrong time,
too early, I'd slip behind the curtain, wrap myself in it,

half faded like an image rocking in a chemical bath.
I'd put my nose against the screen and smell rust

and the scent of cool dirt rising from tulip beds
below where grandma dug star weeds with a trowel.

Of course, I worried. I thought the world, so thick
with leaves and green air, could close up, not let you

return to that space. I could go to the window
again and find you precisely not there and pick at the paint

peeling in the window sill like a cool burn. I hang there,
milky film over water, the symbol for wait,

a thrown powder, hovering in the room long
enough for the blue car on gravel, for the engine

stop, for the metal sound of closing the door,
and all of it in twilight sinking around us like talc.

All my fingers are safe. Nothing is on fire anymore.
I'm covered in feathers at last.

The Sheen on Water

A silhouette of birds lifts into the overcast
and flutters there like a whistling sheet.
In the yard, yellow apples hang like old breasts,
bright lamps in the bare tree, dripping with rain.
The grapes hang too on the wire fence, soft
and over-sweet this late in November, so close
and detailed.

        Grandma teetered in the kitchen as she lifted
the Hamm's can overhead to get the last. It is the idea
of her, no longer distinct but generalized like those birds.
I'd feel better if it were even light.
The snow was falling. The sky was clear.
I was in the next room, watching, munching olives,
staring past the lace curtains at the haze,
at the Rambler parked in the street, at the sparrow
decorating twigs of the maple out front,
the branch swinging under its small weight.
Everything disappeared around me.

I've made a single thing out of the many,
and even that is the sheen on water. When I turn,
it is just water, clear and cold, a bit of cotton, floating.
Where are the birds? Where is that one breath of snow?
That groan as her feet shuffled across tile?

Thresher

The iron teeth of the thresher
cut the earth and air behind the mottled horse
and its slow trot. Sal sits in the rusted chair,
holding tight to the flapping reins,
her dress soiled, frantic before the storm.
Around her, dust blows, fragrant and bright,
like the spiral trellis of jimson she holds in her mind,
imagining those white flowers
as she holds her face from the dust.

Silver everywhere,
fish swim through the sky like white sticks
or pins of gasping. A tin sound clangs far away
as though heard an inch inside the horse,
where all the dark and quiet begins. Sal looks
to the house to see the screen door slap
against the door jamb, to see the bell
blown sideways with its clapper rattle,
brass witness of nightfall and chaos.

Her hair outlines wind as it sifts
about her head, around the ridge of her nose,
and the line of her cheek. Beneath her skin
blood negotiates habitual corners
in her elbow and wrist and silent rooms
in her heart where change is sudden
and unexpected. Inside she says,
"Get done." Inside it is still.
There are sparrows.

Brass Buttons

Her belly's skin moves out and in
with breathing beneath the dark velvet
of her dress held together by brass buttons,
Spanish coins resting in the soft button holes.

Inside the dress, there is wet and warmth,
the body's own weather set against the air,
which slips between the buttons,
underneath the cloth,
and along the outline of her ribs.

She thinks blue music, which reminds
her of this day in 1931 when the heat of Virginia
in summer made her question the boundaries
of her body as she seemed to slip out of her self

like smoke through her dress, which then returns
through the fabric as the scent of dahlias
or the cry of the small dog hidden in the shade
of the rhododendrons and their pink flowering
among the dark and green stars.

Letter from the Alleghenies

I'm in New York now, visiting my aunt
who lives alone on a farm just west
of the Allegheny mountains, a place
I walked for hours and thought
of you as though I were speaking to you,
and with each lunge forward on the path,
I felt the oaks and sunlight move to become
you. How absent I have been since this scarlet
scarf swept through me and changed
the feel of my hips, the way they rise
up into my tongue like fear or desire or the taste
of rust. As I walked, I carried the memory of your lips
in a blue balloon above the ground with its twigs
and periwinkles. Sure, springtime is enough
when I am in love. But otherwise green is
a paltry thing, subject to dismissal like the flies
blowing in the garden behind the fender
of Aunt Zola's junk car. Longing places spring
somewhere between ripening and loss.
If you could see the blue of this sky,
you would wonder why you've stayed away
so long and why the sticks of our bodies
resist and attract in the current of the brook.
Departure means nothing to the spine, but the water
flowing through saddens as the white tufts
of milkweed go vanishing into the shade.
Save some quiet for me. I have so much to say
to you when I return, so much to listen.

Plums

The cool skin of a plum against
the cool skin of a plum.
The sheet of clouds sleeps,
curled over the dark,
and the heavens beyond are filled
with tart juices, the orange fruit,
and the pit so hard

I think it is bone.

Plums in the sink
in a clay bowl
getting clean as water
runs along their edges,
along those rounded bits
of full-throated song.

I arrange them, still wet,
in the basket, and they remain
still and cool, there, through the various
strings of light in the room,
through the various hours.

I take great care with things that fail me.

Nectarine

When the evening looks like jade,
she comes to me, her mouth full of honey,
and kisses me until I tremble,
returning to my body as if falling
from the sky. It is too late to turn
back from this, only so far to go until we are skin
to skin, bone to bone, scraping and drawing back,
like the mouth from the nectarine,
the teeth rattling the washboard
of the maroon stone, dark and new.
It is the center of everything,
and I push toward it with my lips and tongue.

Flavor

The red onion circles into a scent
and snow peas line the white bowl like strips of spring.
This is how the flavors of the world are spent.

While almonds sigh in butter, I'll not repent
my mouth desires the honeyed chicken wing
and the red onion circling into scent.

With luxurious imperfection, lament
the red peppers, the color and taste of a wasp sting
as the flavors of the world are spent.

From small bones the lamb's meat is rent,
then speckled with rosemary and tied with string
while the red onion circles into a scent.

The cool depths of grapes ring resplendent
around the dull tongue of the dead king
where the flavors of the world were spent.

Even the dark hearts of angels breathe content
as the sweet flames of mangoes sing
and the red onion circles into a scent,
the way the flavors of the world are spent.

Water, Flower, Moon

for Matt and Jill

Mornings, they drank coffee on the steps in a concrete
stairwell, I in my lawn chair, books piled beside me.
The light streamed behind her in sheets, sifted through trees
that lined the street. There was always ease between them.
He talked to me, hair disheveled, wearing a bathrobe,
and the orange cat caught grasshoppers with its paws. She read
the paper, summer air washing past her through the screens.
Across the parking lot, Segendra's morning glories
climbed wires a story high, clusters of vines
with purple bells chiming in the heart shaped leaves,
and the sun scaled the maple trees and let go.

Now, these two bodies come to the water to drink
and find the other, mistake the body for water, and fall in,
pulling the drink into their mouths and wanting more.
They are quenched, and the tongue goes dry.
This skin seems enough, the way it wraps around this hand,
this arm, this shoulder and neck. The two uncover a place to stay,
if an animal can be a place. They are two landscapes
moving within one another, she pulling a whole sky
through his hills as he breathes a net of starlings
that iridesce where his lungs meet the heart.
A year happens with all its weather blowing through.
With casual ease, the cloud bank holds a river for weeks.
She opens her arms and lets the rain fall down.

So they come together. She watches him shave in the mirror.
He watches her reading in a chair with the lamplight.
She comes up behind him when he watches the snow fall
in thick clusters that make him dizzy with their tumbling.
They are driving a car late at night past a farm house
with one light on. She is nearly asleep, and he opens the window

to let the air blow on his face. She starts to dream,
and he tastes the warm coffee with his whole mouth,
as a semi passes on the other side of the median. They are driving
home. It is late at night. They live together.

Ten years begin to open, a scroll untied and slowly unrolled,
tiny characters walking beneath a vast mountain
into which they almost disappear in a mist.
But they do not disappear; they are that distance
undulating beside the water in their finery,
memories varied as sand and moss roses
with their succulent leaves filled with honey.

At the foot of the scroll, a bridge vaults over a waterfall.
The two lovers toss magnolia boats over the rail,
white petals billow their sails in a still wind between
the sky and the stream. Later, they sit at a table
laden with fruit in bowls, strawberries sliced
in halves, symmetrical hearts radiating like white
roots to the bright red borders, peppered with seeds.
Cubes of honeydew glisten against a white china bowl.
She takes some melon in her mouth, and it melts there
like green light. She gazes through the shades
and past him to the mountains, mottled with cloud shadow
and the etching of pine trees, dark and low.
She looks back to him, and he looks to her.
The moon rises again into their lives.

Sweet Baby

Your hair dominates the scene, makes mountains
seem like newsprint copies, and the whole valley
is fortunately below you, and your hips keep it there,
huddling in its complacent residential, all those lights
flashing on at the hint of movement. But not your hips.
No, they wait for real movement to turn on like mechanical
bears, the battery slot hidden by explicit fur. You slip like
an eel through the air, blessing all with a hiss
or a gasp, the simple gesture toward our inadequacies—
we are lesser creatures—we die

with the remote in hand. But you possess a broader music,
geologic. The basses carry the melody. We need bigger
kettle drums, a lower bassoon. If you wave your arms
that way once more, I'll turn into the dull branch
of an elm tree glittering with worm holes, tiny moths
grinning with flutter. See, you're just what I need—

someone to make me feel small and alone,
someone to make me like it—light bulb, cattle prod,
your perfume the smell of hair burning in kerosene.
How I long to touch you in the dark. Shelter me with your skin.
Light my way with the tongue of your heart, sweet baby.

II.

Ordinary Girl

Justifying the Ways

for Hannah

Clear from this vantage, how beautiful distance
can be, the intricacy washing out to the sky.
And we are washed out too, our voices

like the click of sticks deep in the woods below,
inarticulate, but sign of some animal we will
not see. I brought you here to balance death with brilliant

flowers, the gentian, mountain forget-me-nots, tiny
blue like flakes from Giotto's vault. I want to justify
my actions, justify your birth into a world of sorrow.

Even your two eyes are reason enough to face it,
and this pine air enough to overwhelm and bless.
I brought you here to live, and the mountains rise

like they were made for this. Come to the edge.
See it shimmer like a saint. We grow huge when we hold
our faces to one another, breathe the same air,

the breath that comes from the other's mouth,
yours, my daughter, the breath of an ordinary girl.

The Scarlet Ibises Have Yet to Arrive

White pelicans at the water's edge erupt in flutter.
Thirty of them turn to glitter, translate horizon
all wrong, yet somehow new and pure as airy bone.
It is like that with birds. One stone instant

the Clark's grebe floats a sinuous black line, then it is
all ripple and beneath. They surprise, showing up
at the spot bordered with tall, furry grasses, so distinct
and moving, dull gold. While there is something disappointing

in spooking the blue heron from behind reeds,
not all loss holds sorrow. I feel something break
with a boom inside. It lifts away, taking
the precision of its beak to the combed line of wing

at the back of its head deep into silhouette, taking its body
into shadow where it dips behind a grass blind in another
channel of water, out of sight, and therefore, gone.
And this is what I've learned, I say to myself,

snow tomorrow. This sky will fill with it
and the musky chatter of frogs eyeing the white flies.

Below the Water

for Jeff and Rachel

I've always loved to look beneath things.
It is not easy to love the surface,
to be dizzied by the light twisting on the water,
and the water, nearly all eye, pulls
at Heaven with gravity and a disregard for time.

The light enters the water and is changed,
the moonlight troubled from the river bottom,
the bruised rose of dawn coloring the current,
the fox pressing its snout below the surface,
receiving water as its pink tongue laps
along the tender crevices of the river heart.

Beneath the sphere of water revolves with gears of eddies,
beneath, the sound the water makes under water,
the white roll of muffled churning
running over logs, over stones, quieting
the sheet of rain that smashes the surface above.

The water remembers the shape of trout swimming
through; it presses along their mouths,
along the blade of their gills. It etches the swing
of the trout fins and the silver-blue net of their bodies
and when the fish have vanished, the water
preserves their image while fresh magic floats inside.

And water is astonished at meeting water,
at meeting other rain with a first and cool touch,
the sediment slowly carried by one stream into the other
where it hovers within, suspended there like longing
fulfilled. Below, something ominous occurs.
Below where the sweep of stars is altered,

where the only sound is the self's whirling and murmur,
the waters of separate storms intertwine,
rush outward toward the world with greater force, amazed.

Staying in Bed

I lie in our bed through the hours of the morning,
reading from a book of elegies and love songs
as I gaze around me at my own lines, writing
themselves into the corners of the room, in the dry flower
laid beneath the picture frame and the candle wax,
pooled at the base of the candle where the night ended
and we began our sleep. It has snowed all night and morning,
and she has opened the blinds so that when I sit up in bed,
I see in the mirror the top of my head and the window
behind me, snow passing through, the trees weighed down.
A crow flies past and drags a dozen squawking grackles behind it.
Two wrens preen themselves in the branches of a pine.

She has made a place for my spirit to dwell,
and I rest there, glass eye in the socket of a doll's head,
balancing the windows and the light coming through.
The quiet of the room says, "There is cold."
It says, "I am shelter."

Waking with Sarah

When Sarah wakes, she draws circles on my cheek
with her small fingers, keeping me awake.
I pull her back down beside me to get her to sleep.
She is two now, and still in diapers, and when I hold her,
I smell the sourness of urine and the sweetness
of her skin. She grabs at my nose and points to my eye,
saying, "Daddy Daddy." Outside, it is still dark, an hour
before actual dawn, but Sarah shows no sign of sleepiness.
She has awakened her older sister, who is sprawled
half-on, half-off the smaller bed beside us, who smiles
when I look to see if she is sleeping, her eyes wide.
Sarah smiles too as she puts her fingers in my mouth.
It should always be this. As my daughters wake,
I wake. When I wake with them, it is morning.

Infant Care

Through some invisible tear, the air
screams. A crazy molecule
at the center of your throat sets
the continent moving like the eye
of a white snake. All the trees
shake. My bones rattle in their drawers.
I've held oceans quieter than you,
little city with your interstates
and steam trains.

You're a pocket of warm weather
stirring in the valley below my ribs.
How many birds do you hold within you?
Whose job was it to carve those wild eyes?
I've been flying with insects so long
I barely recognize my own kind,
though I understand it is common
to find the familiar so strange.
These clawing hands, they cannot be mine,
and they're not. They're yours.

How complicated continuity is.
You writhe like a cat, strong
in these arms that seek to tame you.

Sleeping Inside the Jimson Weed

for Brenda

Close by you're breathing like geese flying in night.
I hear you there but stare past sound into a sky
bludgeoned with stars, foil to dream that finally succumbs.
Now I snore and wake the blankets, which pay close attention
to wrapping us in themselves, alert in their sinuous folds
and the way they shape the air as you and I shift,
willessly like wind in the sheets barely held by wire.
When we wake, there will be canned plums to break

with a spoon, and birds will scratch at the rain gutters
with their feet in the eaves. The flowers that aren't in bloom
will be hoping into the waxy scroll of their buds,
stretching as if opening were the only thing, that beyond
the blossom even the lavender wilting of sleep will seem
to spin wide, to open into a world of wakeful things.

Making Love in the Dark

The room in darkness, the body
in darkness, we are shadows
loving absence. Joy like a jellyfish
floats luminous in the air,
and your mouth is a dream
that drifts upon me, disappears,
then returns with its rhythm
of thirst. We are black snakes,
coiling around and about each other
beneath the earth. We are feathered.
Our hearts rise to where the skin
touches the tongue. A galaxy
appears and whirls about. Stars
begin in my sky and return
to yours. Constellations appear
where there were eyes,
and I kiss you there. We are
a season at night. We are wind
that no one sees, and the electric birds
flying through, leaving a trail of light.

Water Beneath Us

Admit we were there then,
under some less crushing moon,
and the water lit up like that looked less
like a swan's wing than a sweet dirge.
Say you felt the copper sinking in you
the way bare branches draped the trail.
Remember it was wonderful how full of the edge
we were, stepping aside for that tree stump
or the blurred sage burrowing in the shadows.

I kept waiting for some bird to interrupt,
to give us that needle wide
throat from the dark inside
of scrub oaks, waiting for gravel to erupt
as a large animal shuffled its hooves
and tumbled uphill, barely shaking
the sky as it leapt away.

We didn't need birds, but leaned
against a rail of moonlight, on a bridge
composed of black notes held unbelievably long.
One could almost imagine there were two of us,
both of whom were small enough, then, that night
could sip at us and go on in its dry sleep.

I saw silver light and shade through your ribs,
felt a low breeze lift the leaves.
Stars spun through you like winter,
like a cool and sparkling sheet, and you turned
to me to speak, keeping something for yourself,
but unable—at that deliberate hour—
to keep it from spilling out like touch.

Holland Lake, Montana, 1971

We discover what we're made of by turning
to what we've made, the dock, drifting in

the vertiginous lake, the yellow boat carved
into sand and stones. I've been looking

for a rope to tie my hands to keep me in
one place long enough to know where I am.

I've been looking for the terror that takes me.
In the lake, my legs disappear. I breathe needles.

Minnows dart into nowhere and take me there.

Black Walnuts

I should meet you, I'm sure, on another coast,
drink water from ice and admire the winter there,
assessing my state with what I love of desert
that translucent skein of snow over red earth,
and the mention of my daughter, who to you
will seem imagined, real as Perseus or angels,
the black walnuts circling within me, a daughter
of your own growing toward the candle light.

I am not anyone you will ever know,
and I don't know how to change this,
except to meet you again, impossible, close to another year
and come near to telling you I could once have loved you,
and then look away at that angle of light coming
through the window glass across the carpet,
glowing red and gold like the fruit of heaven
and then come close to forgetting it all.

If I'm lucky, I may remember I am alone,
and the world is too much for me, really,
the spoons on the table reflecting everything around,
and me reaching to check the bouquet, the dizzying
light from the chandelier, the warm coffee.
I will think I need no one, if I am lucky,
and we will rise from the table and exchange
a glance that says so, with the inherent suggestion
that everyone in the room is lying, that everyone
in the room would steal a pear if it would help.

Learning to Speak

She learned to speak this way,
the rolling curl of tongue and the hum
buzzing through her thin hair, a scream
that wanders through my sleep where I am
nestled against the wet fur of an inner world.
This is how I've learned to know her.

But I will forget these things—
the sweat on the back of her head
as I pull her from the crib, the blankets
bound about her, clinging tight to her kicking,
the sweet smell of spit on her cheeks
moving and red in the night light.
She calms herself into my arms,
wet and warm and breathing against me.
She opens a liquid tunnel inside herself,
where I turn, where I swim inside a coo,
transparent spider filled with the venom of love.

I remember her entering the room,
her head shining with blood and glue,
her first wondering silence in the air,
then gasp, then sputter, the soft bray
as she slid upon her mother's breast
like a net of fishes, already asleep.
Her head was shaped like a V,
like the angle of her tongue now
as she punctuates the wind with dots.

She is the brilliant flower that bloomed
when I kissed a tree, then plucked the thorns
from my gums, the tiny angel that flew
from the blood, the jewels
spilling out behind her, the unlearned sounds.

Slow

for Sarah

How is it I feel the vague motion of the lake
more when I'm with you and your sister
sitting on these dark rocks, immersed in the scent
of brine? The clouds above that pale slip of island
change, mutate, transform the light slowly
like permanence. But in the water, though I still
the reflection with easy imagination, the sky
is rocking, undulating like the drape on a girl.
It distorts with such clarity that I need to show you
how quickly the world goes, and I turn to you
and you are in another place. A thin light glazes
your eyes, your hair. I want your head absorbed
in my shoulder. I want to feel the whole of your body
physically inside me. It will never be enough.
That hill was in shadow, before.
Now it is fire.

Piercing

I was set against it, for some reason.
"Not until you're ten, and even that
is too early." When she's nine, she calls
from her mother's house and asks,
"Can I pierce my ears?"

Earlier this week, I spent an hour
at the music store, exchanging a rented violin,
the half-sized one she began with
at seven, now too small.

I suppose there was pleasure in handing over
the violin in its case to the rentals clerk
whose desk and counter space were surrounded
by grand pianos, and she took it with little ritual,
though there should have been drums and speeches,
and Hannah should have been there
holding out her arms to show their length as a totem
to her age. I signed the rental agreement
and toted the new violin to my car.

And today, I say, "Yes,"
and she calls later, leaves a message, saying she's done it.
She sounds ecstatic, triumphant in doing
what she has wanted to do for years,
and when I return her call and ask her how it felt,
I somehow feel that she owes me something
because I know something's lost with each wound
we agree to, with each shift into the larger body
of what will simply come. I was even hoping,
just a little, she would say, "Yes, Daddy, it hurt."

Water Damage

That's how they made the temple.
They pounded iron stakes into granite
poured water into the holes. When cold came,
the freezing water cracked the rock.
It's the same with the rain gutters,
pulled lopsided from the side of the house by winter,
tilted sideways so when the ten year rain came, all the water
from one side of the house fell in a continuous sheet
into my basement stairwell, the water overflowing the threshold
into my living room. My daughters huddled behind me,
their hair wet from trying to be in it while water poured
into my rug. I felt it with the base of my feet
cold as a cloud fallen, cold as the memory of ice.
And the rain kept coming, the one time I wanted a storm to stop.
It flowed an alluvial fan beneath the La-Z-Boy and bookcase.
I tried to bail the stairwell with a plastic garbage pail,
but cold water poured down on my head and back,
and my breath caught in a tangle of spine. Thunder crashed;
I jumped inside, dripping on the carpet, electric, safe.

Days later the floor was wet. I woke to a stench, something I hoped
I could avoid. I checked the girls sleeping on the couch, both dry,
then put my nose to the floor and inhaled a swamp,
an odor filled with disease, two-day-old chicken bones, bad fish.
I had smelled something like it before, a scent,
when the woman who was then my wife lay still in our bed
after I had slept two days on the ranch with a friend,
away from her and my infant daughter. There was a smell
in the room like this, and I do not mean to degrade her—
I am done with that—it was just the beginning of decay.

Later I would smell this on her body and know
she'd drunk the vodka she'd hidden and dismissed as some fiction
I was making, even as I held a bottle fresh from her shoe,
and slammed it on the table, and she, drunk, denying it,
glasses on, wearing that silk robe I bought her, and nothing else.
The romance goes out of the body when you smell its death,
that smell as I lay beside her full of desire, squelched
by desire collapsed and furnished with a pall.
The stench of vodka seeping from her pores
poured out from her blood, suspended itself in air
like the Madonna of booze, illuminated
from its dark and searing heart.

As I bent down to inhale the carpet, I recognized the smell,
the fabric mimicking the incense of the body
as it peels flesh from its own bone. Little water, frozen,
pushes at the beaten hole in stone until it cracks,
until it needs only to be covered and dragged from its place.
White towels on the floor soaked up that storm,
the fans blowing a hum into the early dark.
My daughters were so beautiful in their curl of sleep
and more beautiful when they woke. The touch
of their skin keeps me forgetting.

III.

Winged Insects

Winged Insects

I

The fleas dance wildly about my heart.
They deserve iridescence, and I give it.
It must be I am so generous a lord
to acknowledge the particles, the dust motes
that make up happiness, that five star motel.

Yes, I said to the praying mantis, you are
my ideal, the very blueprint of ecstasy, if
only you would spin your green stick body
and set your little hands on fire, mantis, my love,
on fire in my darkness.

II

I bring them all inside. I'm a bottle
of blue flies and wasps, all buzzing,
spinning for escape. This shirt of gnats I am
will certainly explode under the sun's weight,
under its shimmer. Never have so many beetles
been held in one hand, all blue and black and clicking,
each bearing thought in its tin mouth.

My head is a basin filling with wings, black and chitonous—
Oh, these insects are the hardest syllables,
ferocious in their potential. Of course, I must admit
to a certain squeamishness at allowing the wolf spider
to crawl to the tip of my tongue, yet that delightful
little flame when it ignites and burns briefly
at the edge of loss, yes,
that is worth it.

I dream of an enormous moth
that unites us all beyond death, floating, luminous,
blank eyes looking out on nothing.

Eating Flowers

You have only the branches you came with,
and that scent of tea in your mouth. I know
there will be other flavors besides this dust
of cinnamon stick and the acrid roses.
Perhaps the skin will feel different when it soaks
a while in rain filled with tiny oranges and slips
of mint leaves. Then it may seem a refreshing planet,
like an Eden where I can stay. Make flowers of your bones.
Otherwise how will I stay afloat? What will I eat?

You will say a finite number of words with clarity,
and besides you will mean only some. What difference
does it make if I believe even half? I'm in a poor
position among these dark trees stalking you.
I remember when you were a small animal
sitting with its tiny skull on a branch so high up
in this maple that I couldn't have known you were there.
And you weren't watching either. You were a dragonfly
instead, a sting, a bit of water pooled up by the curb
with one knife of sky stabbing from reflected leaves.

The body is cardboard. Let us make of it fire
and breathe in the smoke with our mouths
like the purple, cold lilies beaded with soot,
like the marigold I've saved these years,
like the dried pheasant wing and its bright plumes.

Beating the Drum of a Dead Thing

The carcass of a cow gapes like a leather tent,
like a mouth with rotten teeth. I could crawl
inside it, if I could breathe there, and it would feel
like a cave against this wind, and when I sleep,
my head would push its way into the cow's skull
where I would dream of swimming in a dark, slow river.
I would wake, thinking how dim the desert's become,
that it lacks the detail of sage and red dirt. Somewhere
inside I would realize I was looking out from the wrong
eyes, that mine are clear, not milk blue, with a dust
membrane, dried like the husk of milkweed.

I cannot go near, but I circle it, looking at the bones
like white ships in the red and black sea,
tumbling out in the wave foam. That hide could be played,
but sand would deaden the drum. It would sound more
like beating a pile of leaves with driftwood, not the singing
tone like something that had blood and heart and lungs.
What better arrangement, a hill of peach sand
dotted with low plants, frosted green, and this monument
to the gesture of a cow, final, and hollow like a held groan?
I lean my back into the wind and point my knees toward the cow.
My eyes turn into that wet fire at the edge of the world
where I dance like I'd known it all along.

Bermuda Triangle

I went to this party and all the ones who had disappeared
in the Bermuda Triangle were there, getting drunk.
There was First Sergeant Walter Smith who commanded
the twenty-seventh squadron into the sun, four planes
whose radios all went dead at once, and the last thing
he said to the air was "It is beautiful." There he was, swilling rum
and Coke, holding an unlit cigarette between his thumb
and forefinger, gesturing wildly to some middle-aged gal
in sunglasses. She told him she had been on a cruise with her husband
whom she had grown not to love, especially when he crooned
and played the guitar in the back of the boat as they drifted
over the base of the triangle, and his tropical shirt exerted the fire
of its colors. And behind her, Daniel Malkovich sat
in the corner with a look on his face as though he were
pulling one over on all of us, his black bangs forced
into a curl above his forehead with shining Brylcreem.
I felt like telling him his mother is dead,
that his wife had children with another man and died herself.
And then I felt like telling the Spanish explorer Ernesto Tortosa,
who disappeared with his crew and Spanish Galleon
in 1510 when a soft breeze lifted the boat from the water,
that half a continent is dead, that there is no more wilderness.
I felt like shouting to them all—as they sucked booze from ice,
as they told stories from the great war, as they bragged
about seeing Lincoln in Chicago and leaned toward
one another as though they actually had the bodies
through which desire could have some meaning—
I wanted to tell them that we left the questions of missing things
behind us, that we went on without them.

Drinking

In Ventura, I pour Scotch over ice and splash it
with water. Uncle Terry pours another too.
He looks like you would look if you had lived.
The third Scotch burns less. I use less water
but still swallow without wincing, easily draining
a rattle of ice. Terry lights up a cigarette.
He offers me one. I take it. This is how it would be.
We would drink until one in the morning
and talk our way into a slur. You would understand it all
because you had lived too

                              and I am your son.
If you were real now, you would listen
like Terry, pour me another drink and offer a smoke.
You would wonder again why you drank so much gin
that night in '64 when I woke every two hours to be fed,
when mom woke with me, listening above my sucking sound
for the phone to ring in the kitchen, for the car to pull up
in the driveway, waiting for you to walk over, lean down,
kiss her, then me.

                    She waited for relief as I floated into sleep,
and there was no kiss. It is not you who poured this Scotch,
who lights his cigarette, smoke rising to the chandelier
while I sip the latest in a series of drunks.
But let me pour one for you anyway.
Let me pull up a chair so you can drink with us.
The fact is I don't know what it's like to sit with you,
to see you run your fingers through your hair
then straighten the collar of your impeccably pressed
white shirt. I don't know what it's like to see you move
your lips, saying something to me—
the sound of your voice a new thing.

If you were really sitting there,
I'd be someone else entirely.

But I like who I am now. I like the women I have loved
and my friends. I am glad I live on the plains in Colorado
and not here where you died. It would have been different,
if you had made it home, if you didn't miss the curve
up the road and smash that row of orange trees to pieces.
I am happy now, so forgive me and have one more drink.
Get back in your car and take the same road,
and miss that curve again, but first,
drink your Scotch and listen.

I have a daughter now and a wife.

Elegy of Moths and Song

to Rob Kohler on the death of his father

1

Outside, it is dusk, and the mountains
hold the light longer than the ground
which is dim and shadowy, damp with rain.
Before, I saw a red shafted flicker slip over
the curbside and toward some junipers
where it vanished into the darkening boughs.
It is winter but feels in between,
thirty-five degrees and everything in the valley
melting, mountains like spotted horses,
grazing in the impossible field of twilight.

When I was little, and it was cold,
we skated on the pond at Gibson Park
down by the tracks this side of the river.
I loved to look into the ice to see how thick it was,
to see the brown leaves suspended in it.
When I was lucky, I would see deeper down,
gold fish swimming where there was still water.
I could gaze at them half the day, through
the dizzy strokes of skate blades. I could
hardly believe the fish were alive, seeming
like a gift, something ancient, miraculous.
I knelt and stared as ducks droned
in their wire pen on the island, filled
with the haze of blank elms and bird racket,
floating from the ice.

When I was ten, I walked to school in the dark.
Three blocks away, by the corner store the Coles owned
on First, I could see the top of the smelter stack

rising from the other side of the river, miles away, lit up
like a monument, something sacred in the morning sky,
A crack darkened the uppermost part of its shaft,
and one day after we left town, the city destroyed it,
the detonation so precise that it collapsed into itself.
But those mornings I walked more slowly down that block
so I could just look, so I could think I was in a place
that made the world move like Byzantine around me.

You know winter in Great Falls, those deep nights
when streets are quiet as ice and air is a cold wall.
I shoveled snow two nights after the accident
near Neihart, after I'd seen all five kids reinvented, propped up,
their hands fingering cherry beads like mannequin hands
as the mourners said Hail Marys at the funeral.
I looked up and breathed in the cold with a sting,
thinking, *Where among those stars did they go?*
What could they tell me from there? Below zero
made my eyes ache and water above my scarf.
I scraped the shovel against concrete and heard its echo
smothered through trees and houses on my block
as I sweated beneath winter clothes.
In Montana, it is colder when it is clear.

2

Years later in spring, you came to my house after school,
and we vowed then to be as funny as we could, and later we tried,
biting into the musty peels of bananas at lunch time, tripping on stairs,
then running our heads into lockers or plunging headfirst into snow banks
where we stopped a moment in the deep quiet of fallen snow,
or eating red carnations in a wash of disco and the perfume of girls,
who later we would kiss in the mud by the railroad tracks and the mill.
Once we took off most of our clothes in a snow storm on 25th Street,
waving to the cars, their headlights pouring out snow.
That spring we drank hot chocolate in the kitchen to seal our vow,

and when you left, walking toward Central Avenue, I ran
to the front door and shouted after you, "Don't forget,"
through the screen door, across the lawn, into the budding maples.
The air smelled through with lilac and green.

We were serious that day with our vow, drinking
hot chocolate as though it were an obvious ritual,
arbitrary this time, words at the beginning of friendship
like a glass jar of lilies and violets floating in honey.
Our cups were ringing on the new counter, bits of chocolate
dust drifting at the top as we tasted it in the backs of our mouths.
Perhaps you sensed then that you would lean toward song,
that this was a different vow than either of us knew.
It was the tone and not the intent. It was a vow toward music,
the wall our witness, language my untapped drum
beneath which the water stirred, gathering light,
a blue skein of silk across the collar of a girl.
It was a vow to the content of our lives.

In your mother's church on 2nd North
we gathered all the instruments we could
and set them up behind the pulpit
like a liturgy of brass and wood and string,
your cherry wood electric bass, the frets removed,
my drum set with its silver glitter beneath the finish.
That Wednesday, listening to the empty pews and the mouth
of the balcony opening in the back of the hall,
we played as though we were being told
a secret we knew we were too young to hear.
We listened and played back what we heard clear
to the edge of ourselves where chandeliers
were gleaming with warm frost in the sound.
What gardens we found ourselves afloat in,
the colors of zinnias rising into our throats,
azaleas sparkling in our hands and tongues.
How slow we were to find the endings of those songs.

3

I thought it was a hummingbird, late in August,
that blur darting among the roses on the trellis
in my back yard, hovering near the rhubarb
gone to seed behind the garage. It stalled just enough
for me to see it was a moth, playing a hummingbird
the way nature deceives even those who notice.

In Greeley one summer, with Ann, under pink
alley lights, I found a cecropia moth big as a pocket,
two round eyes like shaded spheres in the dust of its wings.
It lay still in gravel the hue of the rest of its body.
When I touched its wing, the moth ruffled a bit,
then settled back into place, still again, the trees artificial
green in the glow of street lights which buzzed and ticked.
I thought some other summer to see one again.
I thought it was not something I could keep.

Once in Tennessee, I got off the bus in the middle of night
and saw against the truck stop wall a giant moth—I don't know
its kind. It was just huge, big as the inside of my hand.
It was as though a piece of sleep had painted itself
on the clapboard there in the light of one round bulb,
had fashioned itself into a living shadow that made me feel
there was reason to be awake all morning
as the fields and woods filled with luminous mist.
Dark gave way to a pink orange globe of light
that I could look into and not go blind.

4

Last summer at the lodge outside Polson
when you were in Bozeman learning the shape
of your new son, my brother and I played jazz
with your dad in the hot middle of the day.

The night before, we played too, without you,
but with a young kid on bass.
Loving music enough, your dad fumed,
taking only a single chorus on most tunes.
He came to me afterwards and said, "Somebody's
got to keep the time, Joey."

First I retreated into myself,
folded like an ash bag, but then I realized
I missed you that night, how much my music
thrived on you back there keeping the time
and the level of beauty. The next afternoon,
I gathered myself, poured the whole of my time
into jazz, and your dad played out, soloing
on "Georgia," his whole life in his hands and breath.
In the windows behind my drums, a wasp
tapped against the glass. Beyond the windows
Flathead Lake shimmered in its blue and dazzle
like a heaven of water we were trying to gain
with song, thorough, impermanent,
not a trace remaining in the heat of the room.

5

The first time I left my wife I stayed on the ranch with Dirksen.
One night while he was in town, rain clouds came late.
I was inside sitting in a chair with old upholstery.
Hundreds of moths fluttered around the bare bulb
of the ceiling light, brushing their dust on the white paint
as flies buzzed against loose screens.
I heard the rain start. I walked out and knelt
in the gravel driveway, between the small house
and barn, letting the rain hit me and the thunder start.
But then it came close, thunder cracking the sky,
lightning flashing on the cottonwoods,
and the family house, metallic white.

My life torn, inspired by being nowhere,
I stayed only until I wanted to preserve myself.
I went inside to the moths, just listening to the storm,
and the world lit up with peril, real and human,
outside the window. I turned off all the lights in the house.
I could hear cows shuffling against wood fences in the rain.

Our vow did not save us. We wandered
into our lives still loving a joke, convinced of love
with the wrong women, thinking it should be easy.
Our vow did not prepare us for loss. The poinsettias
were Mom's idea. I know they meant little.
It was Christmas, and there were few ways to acknowledge
your grief. I would never try to make you feel better
after having lost a father as I have. I hope you feel
it in the entire beauty of the world.
The other side of silver is ruin.

The Transfer of Heat

At the pool with hundreds, I sit back in a lawn chair,
my heels flattened on white cement.
It is ninety-five degrees, and the heat seems wide,
immeasurable, spread across eight states in one hot gauze.
It wraps around each curve of my shoulders, across
the curve of my stomach. It penetrates the skin. I think
vaguely on some principle in ninth grade science, of heat
touching metal, how molecules are excitable, and the burning
spreads rapidly through solid things, and I am solid, and the heat
moves through. My bones light up with it, and when I look up
to see three gulls riding thermals high up in a perfect sky,
I am translucent. The hills are clear to the feathered stones
of scrub oak and sage, ten miles away, shining detail.

The pregnant woman in the chaise lounge beside me reads a hard back.
In her one-piece suit, she lies back, a blue egg in an incubator, hearing
the language she reads wash over the fetus. The sun keeps warming,
and the child swirls around inside her with an exact digit of lashes,
two thumbs working fluid into a temperate storm. The woman bathes
in the sun, reads a book, and I laze in the periphery of her dream
like a camel or dwarf. The life guard, tan washboard, glances
over the water, boiling with children and their parents in bright suits.
Another in sandals enjoys the talent for twirling her whistle like a propeller,
as she analyzes the shallow end for any disturbance, for something pinned
inside the blue. Certain moments, I am sure I will not die, like this one,
my daughters coming from the waters, wrapped in their own arms,
dripping on me as I hand them their towels. They act cold
as though they are shocked still to be in this other world.
Their teeth actually chatter until their bodies fade to warm,
a gull's cry above, glass needle in the whole sky, aflame with blue.

Speaking

Just to the right of my spine
there is talk. I hear it

like glass blowing in dark
beneath a vein, uncontrollable

chattering, auditioning
for the part in the blue

burn of nerves,
where voices stand at attention

like smoke or imagined
flowers, the idea of neon,

buzzing in the distance
of the skull.

I find them, cool,
little minnows swimming

off in shade, stick creatures,
under water, under stone.

Since truth is a corruption
of possibilities, I am

a narrow water way,
singular, speaking, the electric

eel that I have found
among the moving sand,

inside the white coral.

Foreign Student

He introduces himself first,
standing, against our custom,
saying his name, Bat D. Lee,
Vietnamese, escaped by boat, seventy,
beginning the study of science
and the wonder of America,
though he says none of this except his name
and then continues to stand while other students
fidget, waiting for the moment to end,
to return to the comfort of knowing the language
and the way a class begins. I convince him somehow
to sit, and Laura, pretty beside him, says her name
and tells an amusing story about bad food
and men. Later in the term, he comes to me
for help with his writing. He writes about his home.
He tells me in English not broken like a limb
but filled with static, a signal from far away,
labored and slow, brittle like sticks or bracken,
that the Viet Cong come into his village
and take everything, chickens, bedclothes, jewels,
and they say they will give them back.
Later they come and take the men—
they take everything—to camps, he says,
and we are made to work there, cutting
at the jungle with machetes and no water.
My brother, he tells me, laughs when he works
and a Viet Cong ties his hands behind his back
and holds a machine gun to his head.
Here, Bat shows me. He kneels
on the carpet before me. He forces
his hands behind his back, tight together,
as though twine were bound about them.
I want him to get up. I want him
to sit in the chair across from me.

He explains how the Viet Cong soldier
finds a long stick. Bat holds an invisible stick
to his ear, flattens his palm at its end,
and slams it into his head, still kneeling
on the ground before me. It is spring outside,
grackles chatter in a sprinkler.
On the table my coffee cools.

July in Ballymoney

In a photo in today's news, a father turns
sideways to give a tight kiss to a box.
He seems to carry it with ease as though
his boy were made of paper now, and does not,
in this physical form, possess the psychic weight
that closes the eyes of this father, who wants
his son's body to force him to the ground.

There is a certain obscenity about this picture,
as though on the front page they had shown
a man and woman just fucking, unaware
of the photographer who had found the angle
that he wanted, filled the frame, feeling both the palpable
grief before him and the exhilaration
of capturing that electric sadness on film.
And there it is before me, this colored bit
of newsprint twice as thick as air, this great moral
dignity. Beneath the bright double mirror
of water, a man mourns his sons for every man.

In graffiti on lower Ormeau Road a Catholic wrote
to the Protestants, "What part of *No* Don't You Understand."
No body. *No* hope. *No* time. *No* one. *No* more. *No* opens
like a great black flower that obscures the heat of those flames.
No permeates the brain with its perfume. *No* makes the body
light and permanent, spreads out its seeds and turns the season
back to winter, sweltering, green, but everything else dull white.
All the joy in the world wilts into a cold and snowless wind.
No is held against *no* as someone holds onto that world.

Earlier this week they ran the photo of the boys,
Richard Quinn, Mark Quinn, Jason Quinn,
whose names I say aloud now to make them more real
the way I read the names from stones and their dates

in order to make me feel better about what is left
when we go. And their brother Lee, who stayed
the night at a friend's and lived, who in the picture
is cropped out, so we see only his chest behind those others,
says, "I wonder could they have jumped out
if they woke up earlier." Earlier, we would
have all jumped, earlier before the window shattered
and the Molotov cocktail spilled flames around the bedroom.
Because earlier is always before and things are always
different earlier when things have time to be saved.

Scarecrows

I should write it with water, write it with tea,
something not so permanent as grief, a fragment
of skin maybe. I was sleeping there in my bed,
I'm sure, and my daughters were sleeping
in the next room, Hannah curled in a quilt
on the floor, and Sarah on the futon, sucking
her blanket.

        I'm sure it was cold in Laramie,
and clear, not so different from here, waning gibbous
rising late over the canyon. And what was different?
What made that noise, muffled like a leather bag?
In the showers after basketball when I was twelve,
all those bodies shone bright in the silver water.
I looked at their penises, I looked at their asses,
Mike with his white skin littered with freckles,
Joe Davidson with his uncircumcised foreskin, the first
I'd seen. What was in those bodies that could threaten?
What was in those bodies that made someone think
that a man loving a man is worse than a man hating
a man, worse than a man killing a man with his fists?

When we were waking, getting ready to leave
for the desert, packing the car, brushing our teeth,
some joggers thought they were seeing a scarecrow,
and they were, tied to a fence, bound at the hands,
its head all broken like a bleeding egg. Matthew Shepard
was in there, somewhere, in the stuffing, in the ordinary straw
of that head. And there must have been a heart in there too,
pumping away consciousness, pulling down the shades,
telling the outside birds to hush, fly away
over the white grass, into the hills we leave.

I was starting the car. I was turning the ignition, waiting for a spark.
I was thinking that everything this morning was bright
and full of color, that the mountains were pretty with autumn.
I should have been thinking the street is less solid
than wind, that there is darkness one inch behind morning.
I should have been checking to see that the girls
were strapped in, that their doors were locked
and closed tight, because, after all,
we are soft as peaches.

Bright Phrase

I think I am several.
—Theodore Roethke

I

The skin is a subtle question,
the mouth, the entrance to blood and bone.
Wind blows through me, and the moon
sets like a dark stone in my lungs.

I am water walking through water.

As the future sparks in my gut, lets out
a cold smoke, tumbling upward,
I hold a flashlight up to it and draw a line
of light along the smoke as it disappears,
and this is how you know me from the air.

II

Inside the river of snails, a coil of moonlight
sings in its sleep like pure venom. The cool
bodies slide against one another, and they click click
their spiral shells above the sound more clear.

The snails could be moths or a column of ivory wasps
spinning upward into a blue, empty sky. Instead they are
probable tongues, wet in hard mouths, disembodied,
each announcing, "I am moonlight." But as I thumb
through the snails and find nothing, I break down.

The prophet finds his hands in the guts of his sheep.

Accident

Sooner or later all things fall to accident.
The Venice Opera House burned today
and sent its smoke above St. Mark's and the mud canal.
Pavarotti mourned publicly though he is next.
"Perhaps it is a phoenix," he said with hope.

The red velvet seats turned orange with flames,
and the curtain went up and introduced flames
again and flames behind and flames in the highest
tiers of seating, flames in the opera box where Mussolini
wept while Maria Callas poured silver into the air.
Her letters were there like burning doves,
as were the manuscripts on which Verdi
pressed cold hands, making ink promise sound.

The things we save are the things we think we save.

Fire claimed the space where music slipped
into the world like a new animal, transparent pearl.
Fire opened it, drove it back toward heaven,
that pure neutrality of distance and ash,
that song that stays with us all day.

The Middle of Water

These waters falling down with so much
violence and fury drum a pool of broken
pine and stone. The shade hears it
without listening then colors ferns
with a boom, a green that opens,
moving in wasps. An amber dragonfly
fashions stable air, holds on,
dropping into a current. It catches
a stillness where the whir of its wings
seems slow enough to realize a moment,
before it disappears into a world of trees,
and the water sound hovers a doze.

Ghosts chant beneath the waterfall
in a pattern of falling, in a chaos of falling,
the sound like the wooden Russian doll inside
of which spins another doll and another,
detailed as blue beetles or swans.
When you discover the doll within the doll,
the one outside has changed or hushed—
the bright contours of glaze curled
into vines on which the ruby voices of ghosts
ripen into a howl. The doll inside has changed.
The dolls open themselves. The dolls hold
light like a wind of dahlias inside these waters
falling down with so much violence and fury.

The Sacrament of Roses in Matanzas Creek

I am always this close to perfect silence,
though it helps to be reminded by this shawl
of water, weaving itself about my shoulders,
pulling me in the direction water goes: down.
I keep my spirit still, hanging on a plum branch,
waiting for a stranger to lift me from the white noise
into air more quiet, where I hear
my blood slow, where, like a goddess, I am
born of river, twigs, and sand in my hair.

For the trick to work, I must become less
like water and more like the tree that rises
above the swollen creek. I must learn the language
of living again. I must become my own heat,
abandon the balance of water and limb,
reenter my century with its cars, dirigibles and paper bees.
And when I learn to move my hands again,
draping them over my mother's shoulder
to pick myself up, reaching for the table of roses,
I will remember the dogs barking in the river
and play that sound over in my mind to help
recall how small the body is
in the flood, how near it is
to drowning.

Music's Wife

for Wayne Shorter

Might there have been an echo of self,
blue after-image that lasted, a phrase,
the moment the plane exploded over sea?
Might she have slowly faded like a china bell
rung in the dark, lights visible from shore.
On the other coast he held the soprano sax
in his hands like a Midas-tamed snake,
sustained one note hard against happiness.
The chord resisted until he pulled his lip
from the reed. He looked out on the crowd
as though he could read in the multitude
a sorrow peculiar as flames on a saint,
the fish scattering, the water rising as steam.
To him this new silence sounded like applause.

Marcus Roberts

The blind pianist plays into the windstorm,
bits of white paper whirling in twilight
around the grand. They've turned off the lights,
lowered them to where the dust spins
like sharp air. The crowd hides its eyes
and listens. The wind bellows. The piano
stride blasts away beneath, as though the wind
refers to something else, a conversation
recalled which starts, in memory, to sound
like song. The piano player
may be the only one left when the rain
cuts across the stage. As the sign blows down
and the green trees bend sideways in silver light,
he keeps playing, pushing his head into the space
above the keys, his fingers straddling octaves.
Chaotic gulls scatter in the wind above him.
Behind his eyes a storm blows from deep
like a twin developing the gold glow of nerves
under the skin. The streetlights turn on.
They rock back and forth, pink shadows
waving over the streets.
The cars tick with sand and jazz.

Making Light from Horses

Mark turns off his headlamps, and we tumble
down the dirt road in the dark, fields of wild grass
on either side, just shapes of night. I feel like falling
out of a dream, falling toward my body, a thousand feet
more, tunneling through the darkness, wearing a mask
of stars and speed. Gravel crunches beneath us,
sending up clouds behind like the blur in sleep.
When we finally stop the pickup and go out,
we have no idea where we are, just a sense of which way
to go back, if we want. I stand there in the grass by the fence
feeling burrs in my socks. I hear something bigger
on the other side, something that makes the earth
move deep. Then there is a flabbering of lips, and I begin
to carve the figure of a horse out of night. It comes closer.
I hold out my hand. It pushes its muzzle into the palm,
breathes into me. Its head feels stiff as old wood and hollow,
though I can feel the weight of its muscles lifting my hand.

A certain hum of light comes when one is still,
touching the hide of a horse in the middle of the night,
a pickup still ticking and warm in the gravel beside me.
Everything circles around this group for an instant,
and though it is hard to tell, nothing moves forward.
For a moment there is eternity, something that lasts,
the whole field lit darkly like granite or tracery.
The horse's ears tighten as I run my hands past them into the open
space above its head where my hands seem to rise a moment
like a dust of fire drifting and dispersing into sky. The horse stamps
its feet in the grass, backs away to where I can only hear him,
and then the grass brushes against itself.
The air tastes like Russian olives.

IV.

Requiem

Brahms' Requiem

1

Blessed are they that mourn
for they shall be comforted.

Because this night even the stones in the street
mourn with a low-pitch hum that seems to me
a borrowed groan, I take solace in liquid night,
swirl it in my mouth with translucent spit
where it flourishes like sugar and lime, the taste
the pharaohs loved. I have no place to go
where some burning speck of beauty
will not seek to overwhelm me like the disease
of joy, sparkling, fevered beneath my wind bone.

This sky is no smaller tonight, I say to myself,
realizing I'd hoped it was a hand of flaking skin
I'd scatter as though it were precious, sublime,
because loss most surely should undermine it all.
I will be underground as the water increases its sheen,
and the wind snatches the orange page from the hand of a girl,
pulling it along the blue where it will seem an eternal bird
full of gold flame a finger's width deep. I fall
into the arms of the world, into the cool breeze,
into the animal dirt.

2

For all of flesh is as grass
But the word of the Lord endureth forever.

At the German Deli, Larry tells
of when he was in a trio
beneath a tree in moonlight,

when he slept with a woman second,
already turning her into something like language
as she lay beneath him, pale and blue
in the dark, and the tree behind them
dragged coarse bark into the hour.
Her husband lay on the grass
next to them, tasting the wine
on the inside of his cheeks
as the stars drifted in his sleepiness.
He looked up at them, finding it easy
to ignore infinity completely
for an oncoming dream, ignoring
Larry making noise like a horse shifting
in the grass beside him, saying nothing,
like a fly in amber, like an angel,
like a missing link in the sideshow,
like that train at the turn of the century.

I see the future in the raucous jay,
flitting from the low juniper to the top
of the tennis court fence. On the patio of the pub
Margot talked of quail pie in Scotland,
five quails fresh from the shell,
browned and crisp on top of pastry,
like fried bread with bones in delicate curls
that you can swallow and still breathe.

I know the stories—I followed them through
as I viewed the young woman sweeping
the sidewalk outside the coffee shop,
sweeping piles of grass and cigarette butts,
and swaying inside her dress, beautiful
animal, creating a wind inside her leopard skirt
holding in it the body's perfume.
I imagined a future, there, full of flight,
the arc of her ribs, the strap of her bra,

the way her kiss would move through me
like cool liquid in the IV when I was bound
to be cut open by surgeons I'd never see,
but it always ends with tiny carcasses
smaller than a tongue, brittle and still.
She swept and my frail, sinuous double
became air around her, fell over the lawn,
pretended it truly had skin like the blue jay.

3

Behold thou hast made my days as an handbreadth;
and mine age is as nothing before thee.

No wonder Eliot hated spring
with its gaudy rituals. Right now
outside my windows, cherry blossoms bloom
so richly that the clear air nearly gags and coughs.
What a distraction the world makes of itself
when we should be thinking *the body goes, the body goes,*
the socks I'm wearing have turned to hose.

The poppies riot against the shade, yellow and thin
as a fly's wing, floating through the hour like a line
of music through the back of the brain. It is raining
light there, and the black birds are cheering the end
of geologic time and the triumph of all those that perish.
The poppy revolves in an undistinguished wind
like a brief planet, like a starling disappearing
over the lake, like a bee on a marquee in Vegas.
Turn off the lights, dear, and we'll see what happens next.

4

My heart and flesh rejoice
in the living God.

You said you could go on touching me all night,
as though your hands could be separate from your heart.
When you left, I felt your touch in my sleep, lingering,
delighting the knee, a forest of cherry trees blossoming
at once, nearly waking me with white fire and invisible
smoke. I kept dreaming instead and felt the storm clouds
erupt beneath my shoulders, the skin with its cricket
singing inside it a song the shape of your breath and mouth,
and the air filled with rain and white petals and thunder.

From time to time our spines will join like the two wings
of an electric bird, floating above the shadows of the furniture,
and every cell remembers the salamander and the ape,
and every cell holds the code for fishes, all those bright bodies
darting yellow and blue through water of the future, all those
tiny sets of teeth. See where my body rises to meet you.
My heart lives in every part of it, in every place I have seen,
have tasted in my mouth, have placed on my tongue,
and swallowed. It seeps into either side of midnight.
It hangs there like a net of foreign stars.

5

Your joy no man shall take from you.

I will comfort you
as one comforted by his mother.

I predict a future when the swarm of bees will slow
their churning in the sphere I will form with my hands,
and you will bathe your eyes in warm water

still as moon, transparent as low sound.
I will try to remember you are there, though
you will seem like warmth alone, static absent,
sleeping dove made entire by air. If you speak,
it will be my flesh stoking the billows of joy
that escape and return beyond the skin. I'm taken
with you disappearing in my arms, complicated lamb,
street that holds the heat all night and in morning is silent
but for a light that illuminates you from the side,
but for small birds drinking up the ground,
making melody that blends the closing shade.

6

For we have no continuing city.

We shall not all sleep but we shall be changed.

All the traffic lights in town change at once,
and all the taxi drivers blink in their insomnia
and complacency at each having driven
the same customer to a destination bathed in mums,
lit with brake lights and brass reflections
from the saxophone band, playing over and over
Parker's "Just Friends." It is one in the morning,
and the champagne will never stop flowing,
and the kiss lasts an eternity. How strange; it stays wet,
and the gown on the young woman stays wrinkle free,
and shines like a fish on ice. Pleasure is only pleasure
that remains, the dish boy smoking a cigar,
lit, bright orange as he inhales by the tall house plant,
the smoke rising like the drapery of Samothrace in the Louvre.
They've given away all the fried oysters. There are no more
anywhere to give, and jellyfish swim in the night sky.
"Aren't they beautiful," someone exclaims again,
and "Would that it would never end," she repeats

in a sweet whisper that rivals the leak in the faucet,
they've been complaining about for years, but the clocks
all are flashing and the birds never land.
Heraclitus takes out a pen and stains the water in the pail.

7

Blessed are the dead...

Out on the grass the light was yellow,
the dogs barked like taxi cabs,
and Elvis got down on one knee,
while in their tuxes, the masters of ceremony
from the animal shelter benefit looked on,
grinning. Elvis with his belt buckle
and plastic jewels, knelt down on stage,
moaned like the king of the dead,
his brown hair dyed black. "The sideburns
are real baby. They're real like everything else."

He held out his red cape. Viva Las Vegas.
Viva Elvis. No lights and the sun was going down.
I looked up from the drums and saw the mountains
through the trees, through the crowd of twelve.
The peaks loomed into the late hour of twilight
like granite clocks, like strings through the forehead
and out the back, like a string of absolute gold,
original cold, steadying itself in my throat, steel
willing to support the air but instead
is the skeletal structure for the seconds. Elvis unclean,
Elvis dead but duplicated like a duck call,
like Will Rogers at the cultural center,
like Aunt Madeline's cubism, like the only thing
we have that can remain is a wasp nest,
a storm of gray paper filled with what it's made of.
Elvis said, "Uh huh." Elvis said, "Well."

A terrier barked on a leash. The living have it all.

...and their works do follow them.

These snail shells, white and perfect,
ghost spirals blend with the dirt. How simply
they mark the place where something else has been.
I have put my mouth there and there by the ivy.
Here I sang so no one could hear me.
Here I plucked the violets. They tasted more bitter
than their scent. The little deaths I sang.

At least the world is luminous in contrast with things
that disappear while we look. I took my daughter
to the cattle show, and we looked at Jersey cows,
so tan and beautiful as they chewed hay left
on the concrete floor. All around we heard the shuffling hooves
and the moos coming from clay mouths. It is gone.
My daughter remains, her body shining in the dark
like my third arm, like my second face, smiling
on the other side of town, in the gymnasium,
in bed at her mother's house, in amber with the flies,
the exotic fish and the ferns.

Hold out your hands and show me your eyes.
I've been watching for days, and have finally found
the place your skin gives way to solace,
the place the mountains crumble into at the end.
where they instantly rebuild themselves
and put on again the finery of simple light.
Maybe desire is the Ptolemaic star, and cherubim
stroke the atmosphere of the firmament.
If you're looking for permanence, hold your lips
to the flame my eyes have been, hold your tongue
where my mouth swallowed when you spoke,

where the flavor of cherries and plums dissolves
into something like liquid thought, humming.
Hold out your hands. Carry me an hour.

Want

Sing as though we were only dirt. Sing as though
the texture of plants cannot be improved upon,
as though the color of that frond of juniper
has never been lit so.

On this side it would be the same,
whether there were heaven or not. These are the bodies
of mystics, and this the season of saints,
even with these trees hung low with seed pods,
and katydids popping like tongues in leaves.

Sing as though, regardless, you want more.

THE WHITE PINE PRESS POETRY PRIZE

The annual White Pine Press Poetry Prize, established in 1995, offers a cash award of $500 plus publication of the winning manuscript. Manuscripts are accepted between July 15 and October 31 each year, and the winning manuscript is published the following spring. Please write for additional details.

1998   *Winged Insects* by Joel Long
        Selected by Jane Hirshfield

1997   *A Gathering of Mother Tongues* by Jacqueline Joan Johnson
        Selected by Maurice Kenny

1996   *Bodily Course* by Deborah Gorlin
        Selected by Mekeel McBride

1995   *Zoo & Cathedral* by Nancy Johnson
        Selected by David St. John

Joel Long received an M.F.A. in poetry at the University of Utah, where he studied with Mark Strand, Eavan Boland, Larry Levis, and Jacqueline Osherow. His poems have appeared in numerous publications including *Prairie Schooner, Northern Lights, Sonora Review, Poem, Midwest Quarterly, Wisconsin Review, Mid-American Review, The Sun: A Magazine of Ideas, The Chattahoochee Review,* and *Cape Rock.* He teaches creative writing and art history in West Jordan, Utah, where he founded the Lake Effect Writers Conference.

About White Pine Press

Established in 1973, White Pine Press is a non-profit publishing house dedicated to enriching our literary heritage; promoting cultural awareness, understanding, and respect; and, through literature, addressing social and human rights issues. This mission is accomplished by discovering, producing, and marketing to a diverse circle of readers exceptional works of poetry, fiction, non-fiction, and literature in translation from around the world. Through White Pine Press, authors' voices reach out across cultural, ethnic, and gender boundaries to educate and to entertain.

To insure that these voices are heard as widely as possible, White Pine Press arranges author reading tours and speaking engagements at various colleges, universities, organizations, and bookstores throughout the country. White Pine Press works with colleges and public schools to enrich curricula and promotes discussion in the media. Through these efforts, literature extends beyond the books to make a difference in a rapidly changing world.

As a non-profit organization, White Pine Press depends on support from individuals, foundations, and government agencies to bring you important work that would not be published by profit-driven publishing houses. Our grateful thanks to the many individuals who support this effort as Friends of White Pine Press and to the following organizations: Amter Foundation, Ford Foundation, Korean Culture and Arts Foundation, Lannan Foundation, Lila Wallace-Reader's Digest Fund, Margaret L. Wendt Foundation, Mellon Foundation, National Endowment for the Arts, New York State Council on the Arts, Trubar Foundation, Witter Bynner Foundation, the Slovenian Ministry of Culture, The U.S.-Mexico Fund for Culture, and Wellesley College.

Please support White Pine Press' efforts to present voices that promote cultural awareness and increase understanding and respect among diverse populations of the world. Tax-deductible donations can be made to:

White Pine Press
P.O. Box 236, Buffalo, NY 14201